Jobs for Dogs

Julie Haydon

Some dogs have jobs.

This is Abby.

Abby is a guide dog.

When Abby was young,

she went to school

to be trained as a guide dog.

Today, Abby lives with Sarah.

Sarah is blind.

Abby acts as Sarah's eyes.

Abby knows when it is safe to guide Sarah across the road, and where it is safe to walk.

Abby can guide Sarah safely onto trains, buses, or trams.

This is Dozer.

Dozer is a police dog.

When Dozer was young,

he went to school

to be trained as a police dog.

Today, Dozer lives with Tony.

Tony is a police officer.

Dozer helps Tony do police work.

Dozer knows how to find and fetch things.

Dozer knows how to chase and catch people.

This is Callie.

Callie is a sniffer dog.

When Callie was young,

she went to school

to be trained as a sniffer dog.

Today, Callie works with Luke.

Luke works at the airport.

Callie helps Luke to check bags.

Callie uses her nose to sniff out dangerous things in bags and parcels.

This is Lad.

Lad is a sheep dog.

What is Lad's job?